D0860326

TRAILBLAZERS OF THE WEST

# PIONEERS
## *Adventure in a New Land*

★  ★  ★

Linda Burnett

HIGH
interest
books

Children's Press®
A Division of Scholastic Inc.
New York / Toronto /
Mexico City /
Danbu

0 0022 0295289 7

NRC CASS COUNTY PUBLIC LIBRARY
400 E. MECHANIC
HARRISONVILLE, MO 64701

Book Design: Mindy Liu and Mikhail Bortnik
Contributing Editors: Matthew Pitt and Shira Laskin
Photo Credits: Cover, pp. 4, 23, 31 © Corbis; pp. 7, 18, 41 © Library of Congress
Prints and Photographs Division; pp. 8, 11, 17, 25, 29 © Bettmann/Corbis; p. 20 ©
Roy Morsch/Corbis; p. 26 © Gianni Dagli Orti/Corbis; p. 32 © Nebraska State
Historical Society; pp 36 © The Bancroft Library, University of California,
Berkeley (BANC PIC 1963.002:1440:5--A, BANC PIC 1963.002:0280--FR); p. 38
© Minnesota Historical Society/Corbis

Library of Congress Cataloging-in-Publication Data

Burnett, Linda.
    Pioneers : adventure in a new land / Linda Burnett.
    p. cm .— (Trailblazers of the West)
    Includes index.
    ISBN 0-516-25127-9 (lib. bdg.) — ISBN 0-516-25097-3 (pbk.)
    1. Pioneers—West (U.S.)—History—19th century—Juvenile
literature. 2. Frontier and pioneer life—West (U.S.)—Juvenile
literature. 3. West (U.S.)—History—19th century—Juvenile
literature. I. Title. II. Series.


F596.B95 2005
978'.02—dc22
                                            2005000522

Copyright © 2005 by Rosen Book Works, Inc. All rights reserved.
Published in 2005 by Children's Press, an imprint of Scholastic
Library Publishing.
Published simultaneously in Canada.
Printed in the United States of America.

CHILDREN'S PRESS and associated logos are trademarks
and or registered trademarks of Scholastic Library Publishing.
SCHOLASTIC and associated logos are trademarks and or
registered trademarks of Scholastic Inc.

1 2 3 4 5 6 7 8 9 10 R 14 13 12 11 10 09 08 07 06 05

# CONTENTS

MISSISSIPPI RIVER

# INTRODUCTION

By the mid-1800s, much of the land in the eastern half of the United States had already been settled. Americans had built thousands of homes east of the Mississippi River. Large cities and towns were prospering.

West of the Mississippi River, it was a different story. Although the vast wilderness had been part of the United States for a half century, it was still mostly untouched by settlers. Tall mountain ranges poked into the sky. Empty deserts seemed to stretch on forever. Wild animals roamed the forests and plains.

This was about to change. Beginning in the mid-1800s, countless Americans traveled west, hoping to start new lives. They are

*By the middle of the nineteenth century, many eastern towns such as Memphis, Tennessee, were growing rapidly.*

known as pioneers. For these young travelers, the unexplored western territory represented their future. They were thrilled to journey west. Yet they were also filled with uncertainty, and even terror.

These brave pioneers left the comfort of their homes in search of new opportunities. The trip was not always easy, though. Many pioneers grew ill from diseases. They trudged through severe weather, with very little shelter to protect them. For some pioneers, the voyage ended in death. Those who survived the journey knew their hardships were not over. They had to build their own homes, make their own clothes, and grow their own food. For these early settlers of the West, each day was filled with many challenges.

*Thousands of pioneers braved the journey west with hopes of better lives on the frontier.*

▶

# CHAPTER 1

# HOW IT BEGAN

## A New Nation Grows

Thomas Jefferson was the third president of the United States. In 1803, he bought the Louisiana Territory from France. This is known as the Louisiana Purchase. The U.S. government paid $15,000,000 for more than 800,000 square miles (2.1 million square kilometers) of land. Parts of fifteen current states come from the Louisiana Purchase. In one bold move, Jefferson had doubled the size of the country.

Much of the land of the Louisiana Purchase had not been explored. One year later, in May 1804, President Jefferson sent Meriwether Lewis and William Clark to explore this frontier and report what they found.

*The U.S. government bought western lands from France in the Louisiana Purchase. Here, a French official hands papers to an American official during a ceremony for the purchase.*

Lewis and Clark put together a team of men to go with them. Starting from St. Louis, Missouri, at the Missouri River, Lewis and Clark's goal was to reach the shores of the Pacific Ocean. The explorers wrote about their trip in diaries and letters. Their two-year journey brought home exciting stories of unknown plants and animals, encounters with Native Americans, and the beauty of the wild lands they visited. Lewis and Clark's voyage west blazed a trail that many Americans would follow.

## Who Came West

Most Americans were eager to expand their nation's borders. They felt that their country's western border should reach the Pacific Coast. For some, expanding national borders was a way to spread American values. Others saw the new fertile land as a way to make their living. These people were eager to settle the new region.

The first pioneers to take advantage of the new land were called voyageurs. Companies hired voyageurs to hunt animals, such as beavers, for their fur. The men worked hard transporting the valuable furs to faraway locations.

*Lewis and Clark were guided across the West by Sacagawea, a Native American woman (shown pointing). She led the explorers through the wilderness and made peace with the many Native Americans the team encountered on their journey.*

Most of the pioneers worked in cities or on farms. The fertile land in the West attracted them. Many of these Americans were poor and believed that heading west would give them a chance to improve their lives.

## The Wagon Trail

The pioneers started to travel in covered wagons by the 1840s. Since there was safety in numbers, pioneers usually traveled in large caravans, or groups, of wagons.

Pioneers had a choice of several routes for their westward journey. These trails included the Mormon Pioneer Trail, the Overland Trail, the Santa Fe Trail, and the Oregon Trail.

Most pioneers traveled on the Oregon Trail. This trail started in Independence, Missouri. It wove across Kansas, Nebraska, Wyoming, Idaho, and Oregon. The trip took the adventurers through the Rocky Mountains. The journey from Independence to the final destination in Oregon City, Oregon, was about 2,000 miles (3,218 kilometers). The trip usually took about six months.

These various trails were known as transcontinental highways. Over the years, the wheels and animal hooves of thousands of wagons wore out the soil and grassy plains they traveled. The tracks they made created trails that guided pioneers to their destination.

Pioneers had very little storage space in their wagons. Each item they brought with them had to serve a purpose. They crammed furniture, cooking utensils, and clothing into the wagons. They brought guns and ammunition to hunt animals and protect them from attacks.

*In 1843, the first large group of pioneers began their journey along the Oregon Trail. About 1,000 men, women, and children made the trip together.*

The pioneers traveled from sunrise to dusk. When they stopped to rest, they formed a corral with their wagons by arranging them in a circle. This gave the pioneers protection against an attack. Inside the corral, they cooked simple meals over a campfire. The pioneers used basic ingredients, such as flour, bacon, beans, and dried fruit.

At night, the pioneers slept outside their wagons, since the wagons were stuffed with supplies. It wasn't easy to get restful sleep.

## ⋆ FRONTIER FACT ⋆

Pioneers were allowed to bring very few personal items on their journey. Full wagons could not weigh more than 2,400 pounds (1,088 kilograms) each. That's about the weight of a compact car. A horse or ox pulling the wagon could not pull anything heavier.

The nights could get bitterly cold, and the pioneers had very little clothing to keep them warm. Also, without much shelter, they were easy prey for any wild animals in the area.

After they made it through the mountains, the pioneers headed north of the Great Salt Lake. At this point, some pioneers split off from the trail and changed direction. These pioneers were often in search of gold in California. They took the California Trail, which went across the Nevada desert and through the Sierra Nevada Mountains. Those who stayed on the Oregon Trail kept heading northwest, along the Snake River.

# THE FRONTIER: PROMISED LAND FOR ALL

In 1877, a former slave named Benjamin Singleton called on African Americans to head west to Kansas. Though the American Civil War had ended, Singleton knew that many former slaves were still being mistreated. Racism continued to be a major problem in the United States. Singleton thought the West could be a land of opportunity for families of all backgrounds. His call was certainly answered. By 1879, fifteen thousand African Americans tried to make a new home on the prairies of Kansas.

People from around the world came to settle in the American West. These people included Germans and Scots. Around the 1880s, Chinese and Jewish families came to the United States to seek new homes as well. Almost all of these people were poor. They did not have communities or groups of friends to assist them during their voyage. Worse, they did not speak English, which made their travels even harder. For them, though, the great opportunities offered in the West outweighed the risks.

## Home Free

Early pioneers had few possessions and very little money. On their own, these pioneers probably would have failed to settle the West. This is why it was important for the U.S. government to give support to these early settlers. The government passed laws that encouraged men and women to journey west. The laws also helped pioneers own and settle the land once they reached their destination.

The first of these laws was introduced in 1841. It was called the Preemption Act. This act allowed pioneers to live on and own their own piece of land. In return, they had to work the soil and improve the condition of the land. The government allowed these early settlers to purchase this land for only $1.25 per acre.

The Homestead Act of 1862 did even more to help families get land. Under this law, the head of a family could claim 160 acres (64.7 hectares) of U.S. territory. The family had to farm the land for five years and build a house on it. After that, the land was theirs.

This temptation of free land and fresh starts sent thousands of Americans west. They were eager to become homesteaders.

*Laws introduced by the government allowed pioneers to begin building homes on the western frontier. This 1875 photo shows a family outside their log cabin in Utah.*

A SUPPLY TRAIN IN A SNOW-STORM.

DISTRIBUTING SUPPLIES TO INDIANS.

WINTER LIFE ON THE PLAINS.—Drawn by P. Frenzeny.—[See Page 87.]

# CHAPTER 2

# WELCOME TO HARD TIMES

The voyage west promised great adventure. But it also involved great risks. One of the biggest risks was dealing with the many challenges of nature. Hail, driving rain, and high winds pounded the pioneers' thin wagon covers. Freezing temperatures could make a wagon feel like an icebox. Blistering summer heat could turn that same wagon into a sweatbox.

Pioneers learned to read the sky for oncoming tornadoes. If they got in the path of a fierce twister, they could be killed. There were often terrible dry spells in desert areas. If a pioneer was careless in setting a campfire, the dry prairie grass caught fire. The dry land would go up in flames, forcing the pioneers to flee.

*These illustrations from* Harper's Weekly *magazine appeared on February 11, 1882. The top image shows a wagon train traveling through a snowstorm. At the bottom, the U.S. government is shown giving supplies to Native Americans in the West.*

But the severe weather conditions were only one element of nature that threatened the pioneers. Another came in the form of the wildlife that lived on the western frontier.

### Animal Trouble

One unusual form of wildlife that made pioneer life difficult was the grasshopper.

*Swarming grasshoppers made life difficult for the pioneers.*

During some years, grasshoppers invaded the western plains by the millions, destroying crops and trees. Early farmers tried everything to stop the bugs. They built traps and burned sulfur to keep the bugs from ruining their crops. A local newspaper in Nebraska called the *Homesteader* reported on this plague: "The air is filled with them, the ground is covered with them, and people think and talk of nothing else. It rains grasshoppers and snows grasshoppers."

Pioneers dealt with more than a strange flood of insects. They often came face-to-face with wild animals. Grizzly bears, wolves, and buffalo freely roamed the West. The pioneers hunted these animals for food and fur. Sometimes, however, the animals turned the tables, and killed or ate the pioneers.

Starvation and illnesses were a constant threat to pioneers on the trail. Measles, mumps, smallpox, and fevers could strike a caravan at any time. A bad illness could weaken or wipe out the whole group. The pioneers were often defenseless against such diseases. They had little or no available medical care as they traveled the trails.

## America the Beautiful

Danger and hardship were facts of life on the frontier. But anxious and weary pioneers were also rewarded with amazing scenes of natural beauty. The lush grass of the prairies stretched on for miles and miles. In southwestern deserts, the pioneers witnessed sandstone walls that changed colors with the seasons.

The Southwest was also the site of unusual rock forms, such as mesas. Great canyons dug deep into the earth like giant bathtubs. In the Pacific Northwest, vast pine forests astonished pioneers. A rich and endless blue sky hung above these great wonders. Watching the Sun rise and set against the mountains or plains could send their spirits soaring.

## Anxious Arrival

When the pioneers first arrived at their destinations, they had to face some hard truths about survival. To succeed in their new land, they would have to rely on their courage and skills. There were no settled towns. There were no stores to shop in. The pioneers didn't have paying jobs that they could count on for money. What they did have was land that they could claim and use as their own.

*Beautiful sights, such as this desert on the border of Arizona and Colorado, helped lift the pioneers' spirits.*

But there was a catch. The soil had never been farmed. There were no crops lying beneath the soil, waiting to be plucked from the ground and eaten or sold. Being the first settlers in this new land, the pioneers would have to do everything themselves.

## Frontier Fashion

The pioneers usually sewed their own clothing with homespun wool. Buffalo and buckskin were also used to make clothing. Even the canvas tops of wagons were sewn into frontier clothing. The tops could also be used to make curtains for a homesteader's log cabin.

Frontier women had no need for the long, fluffy dresses they had worn in eastern cities. The bottoms of those dresses would only get muddy and wet if frontier women wore them while working outdoors. The women simplified their wardrobes. They shortened their dresses so they did not touch the ground.

## ★ FRONTIER FACT ★

**Women even sewed lead into the hems of their skirts. This kept the skirts from blowing over their heads in the wind.**

Men wore flannel or cotton shirts and short wool coats. They wore high boots to protect their feet from rattlesnakes. These tough boots also protected frontier men from getting stuck by thorns and bushes as they worked in the fields.

*Life on the frontier was far from easy. Pioneers had to be ready for anything—even grizzly bear attacks.*

# CHAPTER 3

# GROWING PAINS

## On the Right Track

The U.S. government wanted to build a railroad system that would connect the East and West coasts of the country. This railroad would help the West grow by bringing goods and services to pioneer families.

The Union Pacific and Central Pacific railroads were chosen to build this railroad system. The Union Pacific laid tracks westward from Omaha, Nebraska. The Central Pacific laid tracks eastward from Sacramento, California. The two lines eventually met at Promontory Point, Utah. The railroad was completed in 1869, about six-and-a-half years after it was started. This was the first transcontinental railroad.

*The transcontinental railroad connected the East and West coasts of America. It also brought more people and businesses to the West.*

The railroad was the fastest and easiest way for people to get across the country. For the first time, the eastern and western parts of the country were joined.

### Trade, Trouble, and Treaties

Not everyone living in North America was thrilled to see the railroad built. Native Americans had lived in these western lands for thousands of years. Suddenly, Native Americans were forced to share this land with strangers. This new situation caused lots of tense moments and violent conflicts.

The U.S. government sometimes tried to protect the land rights of Native American tribes. Yet the government still wanted the land for white pioneers. As pioneers settled the West, they built homes, schools, and businesses. They had no intention of leaving these lands. A brutal and sometimes bloody battle between Native Americans and white settlers soon began.

# AMERICAN BUFFALO

Land was not the only sore spot in relations between pioneers and Native Americans. Plains Indians such as the Comanche, Cheyenne, and Sioux fought the settlers for killing their buffalo. These tribes relied on buffalo for food, clothing, and shelter. The settlers often killed buffalo

just for sport. The Native Americans could not allow settlers to hunt and kill this animal they needed for survival.

## Peace on Paper

To create peace between Native Americans and the new settlers, the U.S. government negotiated treaties. Native Americans were often promised money for the lands on which they lived. In return, the Native Americans agreed to move elsewhere. The idea was to avoid violence between the two groups.

Such peace plans worked for a short while. Yet as more and more pioneers headed west, the violence between the warring groups only got bloodier. Neither side believed they could trust the other. Each often broke the truces.

By the 1880s, Native Americans found themselves in danger of not only losing their lands but of being killed off by the white settlers. The firepower of the settlers was simply overpowering the Native Americans in battle.

To protect the Native Americans, while taking their lands at the same time, the government sent many tribes to live on sectioned-off areas called reservations. The conditions on reservations were usually poor. The land was not as fertile as the Native Americans' natural homelands. Even on the reservations, Native Americans faced violence because warring tribes were often forced to live together.

Sometimes, rival tribes worked together to battle their common enemy. Sitting Bull, a chief of the Sioux tribe, helped fight a major battle against the U.S. military. The chief joined forces with the Cheyenne. The two tribes were attacked by Lieutenant Colonel George Custer and his men at Little Bighorn in South Dakota. All of Custer's men were slaughtered. The U.S. army cracked down on the Sioux and Cheyenne. Over the next five years, these tribes were conquered.

On June 25, 1876, about 240 soldiers led by Custer were killed in the battle known as Custer's Last Stand.

*Early pioneer homes were often made from sod. Families lived together in one room in these simple homes.*

## Creating a Community

Of course, the settlers were not using all of their energy to fight Native Americans. They were also putting down roots in the western territories. Many of them carved their early homes into hillsides. Some used sod to close off the open side. The most expensive material for their new homes was the glass for the window. Each window cost the same as an acre of land.

These homes did not provide much shelter. Snakes and insects easily slipped into them. The roofs of wood and sod were leaky.

The interiors were dark, cold, and damp.
Settlers tried to move into better shelters
as soon as possible. The wealthier settlers
were able to build timber houses with
shingled roofs.

Once they set up their homes, the settlers
tended to the soil. They planted mostly corn
and wheat. The pioneers also dug wells to get
their drinking and bathing water. During the
day, the pioneers exhausted themselves with
hard work. Yet nights were not much better.
Most of these courageous people spent their
nights alone, having left behind friends and
relatives to be in this harsh, strange land.

## Putting Down Roots

For so long, the new settlers had traveled and
lived mostly by themselves. They were eager
to begin to build frontier communities.
Religious functions provided settlers with an
easy way to meet their neighbors. Settlers
quickly built churches. There, families could
gather, meet, and worship. They threw picnics

and Fourth of July parties. Pioneers enjoyed these events. Celebrating helped the settlers through tough times. On the frontier, tragedy was common and impossible to prevent. Crops often failed because of droughts or insects. Settlers died from starvation, diseases, and even common illnesses. Yet funerals were not completely sad occasions. Communities often came together, providing pioneers with another chance to meet their neighbors.

## The Price of Progress

Towns sprang up across the plains. Settlers built houses and shacks throughout the frontier. Day after day, railroads shuttled new families westward. As a town's popularity grew, more businesses appeared. Saloons, hotels, schools, and businesses were constructed to provide more services to the new residents. This progress led to an increase in crime. Rising tempers in saloons often triggered brawls and gunfights. Gambling became a popular pastime in frontier towns. Losing money could lead to rising tempers, and deadly shootings.

Police forces in these towns were not very organized. The government could not control the sprawling frontier. Some people took the law into their own hands. Revolvers and Colt pistols soon showed up in almost every pioneer's hands. Small-time crooks were hanged for petty crimes. Farmers shot each other in disputes over water. This is how the frontier earned its reputation as the Wild West.

*Settlers often spent time gambling in saloons. They drank alcohol and played cards together.*

# CHAPTER 4

# THE GREAT WEST

By 1890, the days of discovery and settlement had ended. Much of the western frontier had been settled. Just as President Jefferson had hoped, the country's borders now reached the Pacific Ocean. The land was changed from a wilderness to a growing civilization. It only took seventy-seven years to transform an empty region into one with millions of residents. The land west of the Mississippi River was now made up of separate states. Some people said the country was now complete.

## Bigger and Better

While settling the West, the country grew in many ways, not just physically. During this time of growth, American inventiveness was on the rise.

*As towns developed across the West, different groups of people established communities. Shown here are the outdoor markets of Chinatown in San Francisco, California, around 1890.*

Many new farming tools were invented. This equipment included the tractor, cotton picker, and corn planter. Great minds in the West also helped solve farming problems. They learned better ways to plant crops and keep them well watered. The frontier's rich farmland provided food to the states east of the Mississippi River. This allowed the United States to become less dependent on European goods.

The first tractors used steam-powered engines. Farmers used these tractors to pull equipment or materials.

## The Western Way

Historians found that pioneers did not simply follow the lead of eastern states. One historian wrote, "The true point of view in the history of this nation is . . . the Great West." In the beginning of the settlement of the West, there were no social classes. This led to better equality among the races, as well as among men and women. For instance, Wyoming was the first state to allow women to vote in elections. Wyoming passed this law in 1869. Most women in the United States were denied the right to vote for several more decades.

## Natives' Soil

The determination of the brave pioneers to make a new country had its costs. The settling of the frontier came at the expense of Native Americans. Today, there are about three hundred Native American reservations scattered across the country. Unfortunately, living conditions in them are often very poor.

## Frontier Folklore

The settling of the West left a great history. Movies, television, and books keep our image of the West alive. Even today, the West inspires images of cattle, wagon trains, and small houses on the prairie. We are used to seeing gun showdowns by men in wide-brimmed hats or cowboys wearing clanging spurs.

Many Hollywood films featured larger-than-life characters who really did exist. These well-known people helped settle the West and became heroes to their fellow pioneers. William Cody (Buffalo Bill) is one example. He was a hunter, a military scout, and an entertainer. Kit Carson is another folk hero. He guided government expeditions to the West. He was also a Civil War colonel.

Think of what it would have been like to tackle the frontier. Do you think you would have made it across the trail? Could you have suffered through harsh winter nights? Facing risks and dangers with very few resources, the pioneers suffered, but they survived. They made the nation better with will, courage, and faith. Their sacrifices forged the great country we live in today.

*Buffalo Bill starred in* Buffalo Bill's Wild West, *a lively show about cowboys, Native Americans, and sharpshooters. The show was a great success and was popular for thirty years. Shown here is an 1899 poster for the show.*

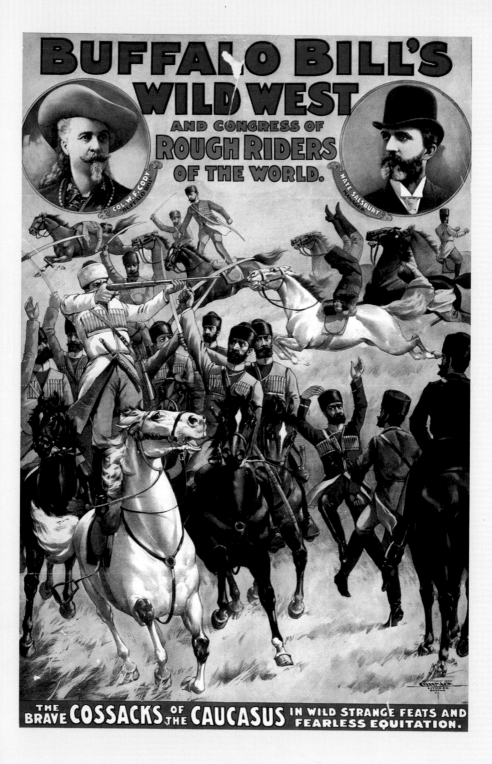

**caravan** (**ka**-ruh-van) a group of people or vehicles traveling together

**corral** (kuh-**ral**) a group of wagons or vehicles arranged together for defense

**homesteader** (**home**-stead-uhr) a person who settled on land given by the U.S. government on the condition that he clear and work it for five years

**mesa** (**may**-suh) a hill or mountain with steep sides and a flat top

**negotiated** (ni-**goh**-shee-ay-ted) to bargain or discuss something with someone so that you can come to an agreement

**plague** (**playg**) a very serious disease that spreads quickly to many people and often causes death

**reservations** (rez-ur-**vay**-shuhnz) an area of land set aside by the government for a special purpose

**smallpox (smawl-**poks) a disease that causes
chills, high fever, and pimples that can
leave scars

**sod (sod)** the top layer of the soil and the grass
attached to it

**sulfur (suhl-**fur) a yellow chemical element used
in gunpowder, matches, and fertilizer

**transcontinental** (transs-kon-tuh-**nen**-tuhl)
crossing a continent

**treaties (tree-**teez) formal agreements between
two or more countries

**voyageurs (voi-**a-jerz) a man employed by a fur
company to bring goods to and from faraway
places

Freedman, Russell. *Children of the Wild West.* Boston: Houghton Mifflin, 1990.

Greenwood, Barbara. *A Pioneer Sampler: The Daily Life of a Pioneer Family in 1840.* Boston: Houghton Mifflin, 1998.

Murray, Stuart. *Wild West.* New York: DK Publishing, 2001.

Wilder, Laura Ingalls. *On the Way Home: The Diary of a Trip from South Dakota to Mansfield, Missouri, in 1894.* Madison, WI: Turtleback Books, 1990.

## Organizations

### California Historical Society
678 Mission St.
San Francisco, CA   94105
(415) 357-1848
*www.calhist.org*

### Fort Laramie National Historic Site
965 Gray Rocks Rd.
Fort Laramie, WY   82212
(307) 837-2221
*www.nps.gov/fola*

### Jefferson National Expansion Memorial
11. N. 4th St.
St. Louis, MO   63102
(314) 655-1700
*www.nps.gov/jeff/*

## Web Sites

### America's West—Development and History
*www.americanwest.com*
This informative Web site offers a history of the development of the West. Learn about cowboys, pioneers, outlaws, and more.

### National Geographic: Lewis and Clark
*www.nationalgeographic.com/lewisandclark*
Visit this Web site for more information about Lewis and Clark's journey west. It includes journal entries, historical photos, and a time line.

### Oregon National Historic Trail
*www.nps.gov/oreg/oreg/history.htm*
This Web site features the history of the Oregon Trail. Use the interactive map to learn about the many trail sites visited by the pioneers as they traveled west.

# INDEX

## About the Author

Linda Burnett grew up in New York City. Like the pioneers, she has since moved out West. She now lives in Los Angeles, California, where she is a freelance writer.